**This book is dedicated to Dan and Colleen.
May God bless you always.**

This book is offered with special love for my family of origin - my parents, Colleen Moore and Walter Empey, my step-father, Jack Schmidt, my siblings, Cathy Posthuma, Mary Eisenga, Bill Schmidt and Johnny, as we remember him. May forgiveness and love fill us as we continue to share our journey through life.

TABLE OF CONTENTS

Chapter **1**	THE BEGINNING - WHAT ABOUT FORGIVENESS	**1**
Chapter **2**	WHY IS FORGIVENESS SO HARD?	**27**
Chapter **3**	RESENTMENTS, HATE, ANGER	**41**
Chapter **4**	WHO AND WHAT DO WE NEED TO FORGIVE	**67**
Chapter **5**	WHAT FORGIVENESS IS AND IS NOT	**79**
Chapter **6**	THE THREE STEPS TO FORGIVENESS	**97**
Chapter **7**	MOVING ON - WHAT HAPPENS WHEN WE FORGIVE	**129**

PREFACE

Someone wise once said, "We teach most what we need to learn." I needed to learn to forgive. I searched for answers and ways to do it and in the process, this book was born. This book is a product of an intense ten year journey to heal within. At times the process hurt deeply but the end result has been freedom, peace, higher self-esteem, knowledge and a healthier new connectedness with myself and others. I still hurt at times, because as life goes on, "stuff" happens. But the old internal fires have stopped burning. The sorrow and tears have ebbed. New behaviors, tools and choices have taken root. I still remember. I still have scars. But they have lost their power They don't control me anymore. Through this process of forgiveness and healing, I have turned my pain into ashes and the ashes into new life.

This has not been a solo journey. I have had lots of strong support and guidance, and without it, I wouldn't have arrived at this place of peace. I could not have done this alone. It was not that I didn't want to. I just didn't know how.

I am not an expert on forgiveness, but I do know a lot about it. I have learned it in two ways. I researched the topic through books, lectures, tapes and people - both professional and non-professional. I also learned about the topic through life and my own experiences. Throughout this book, I will share some of my personal journey to forgiveness. You will know this when you see green ink on notebook paper. Some of you will share experiences like mine. Some of you will not. I don't believe it matters where our pain and resentments come from, I believe the healing process is the same. You may have had a wonderful childhood but have been hurt or abused by spouses, friends or others in your life. Perhaps your entire life has been rosy but you have minor hurts that keep nagging at you. Whatever the source of your pain and resentments, I believe this book and these processes can help you grow in awareness and heal.

Please accept this book as a gift of myself and my research. It is honest. It is sincere. Please read it with a gentle heart and allow it to help you, however it can. God bless.

Maureen Burns

Maureen Burns

the beginning

what about forgiveness...

THROUGHOUT OUR LIVES WE'VE BEEN TOLD:

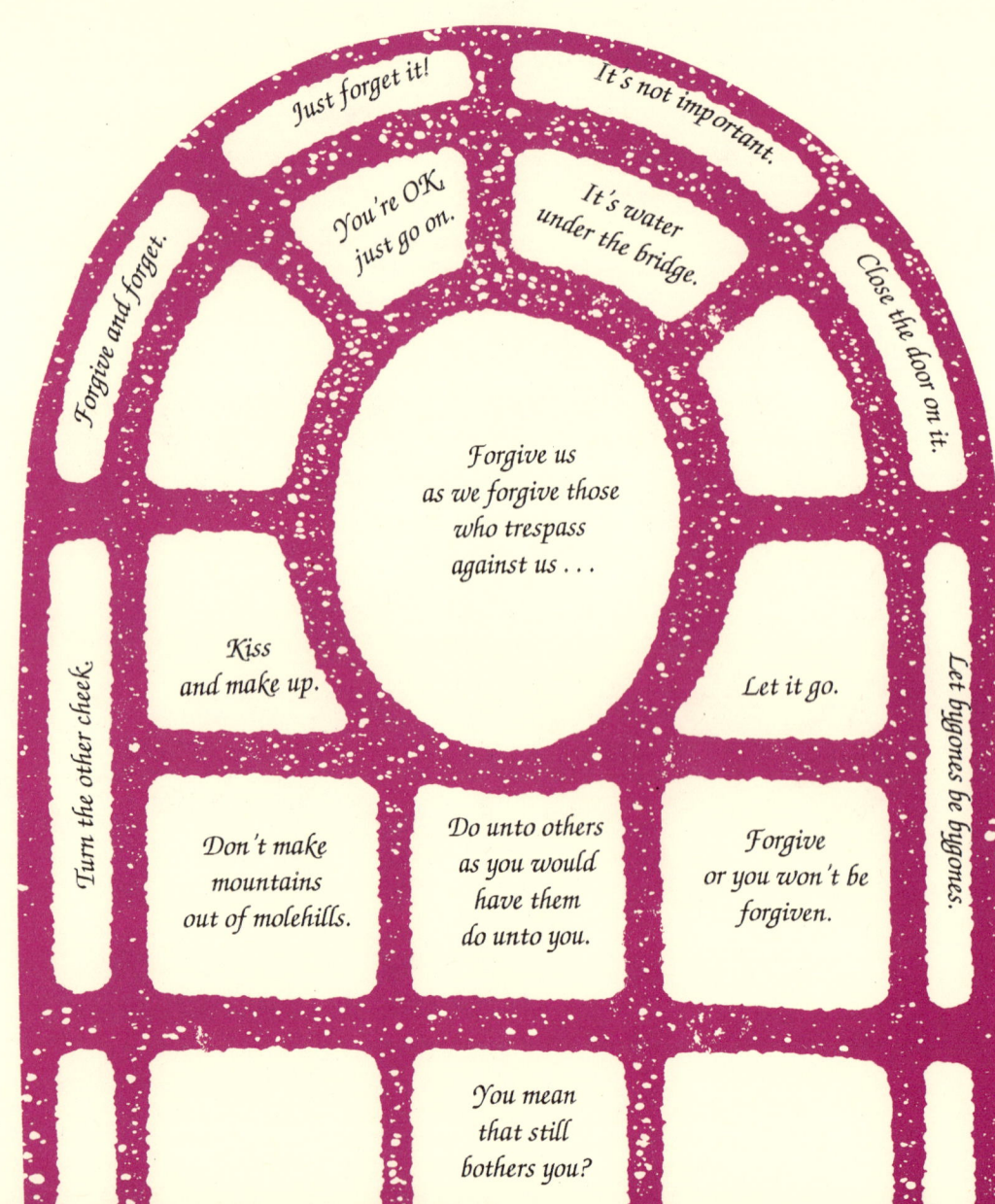

. . . . . but we think:

When we don't forgive, we suffer, and even though we may not want to forgive, we want the pain to end. We want to be healed. We realize we need to stop licking our wounds. It is time.

Sometimes, we know we NEED to forgive;
                                      sometimes we're desperate for it,

but

the reality is

WE DON'T KNOW HOW!

All my life I've been told _to_ forgive, but no one ever told me _how_. I should know by now. I believe I'm spiritual, I've been raised a Christian, gone to religious school, read religious and self-growth books, attended spiritual classes, married a counselor, consulted with counselors, written self-help books and articles and attended self-growth seminars. I think I communicate well. I have a college degree in education and am a professional writer and motivation and communications speaker. Somewhere along the way, I should have learned how to forgive. But I never did. I didn't have a clue. When I finally decided I needed to forgive, I had no idea how to begin. It was a mystery.

"It's easier to confess and seek healing for our own sins than to heal ourselves of what others have done to us.

It is easier to get forgiven than forgive."

Lewis Smedes

"Forgiveness is love's toughest work and biggest risk. It is the hardest trick in the whole bag of personal relationships."[1]

There are *no* magic words

no magic potions

no shortcuts.

Forgiveness can be a long journey.

PAINFUL

takes time

work through unfinished business

deal with feelings

HARD WORK

LET GO

It may not feel good to forgive

but

it feels even worse not to forgive.

Our feelings are the least dependable part of us. They run deeper than reason; and fluctuate erratically.

        We may think we shouldn't feel hurt
        or
        that we should feel hurt.

Either way, we are hurt, and we need to forgive.

        Whether or not they deserve to be forgiven . . .
        WE deserve it.

We deserve to -
    let go of our pain   *feel joy*   *laugh*   *feel whole*
    like ourselves   *get on with our life*   *have peace of mind*
    improve our quality of life   *quit allowing old wounds to hold us back.*

Keeping ourselves a victim feels hopeless and painful.

Is holding on worth the price you are paying? Would you rather be right than happy? Where are you now? Where would you like to be?

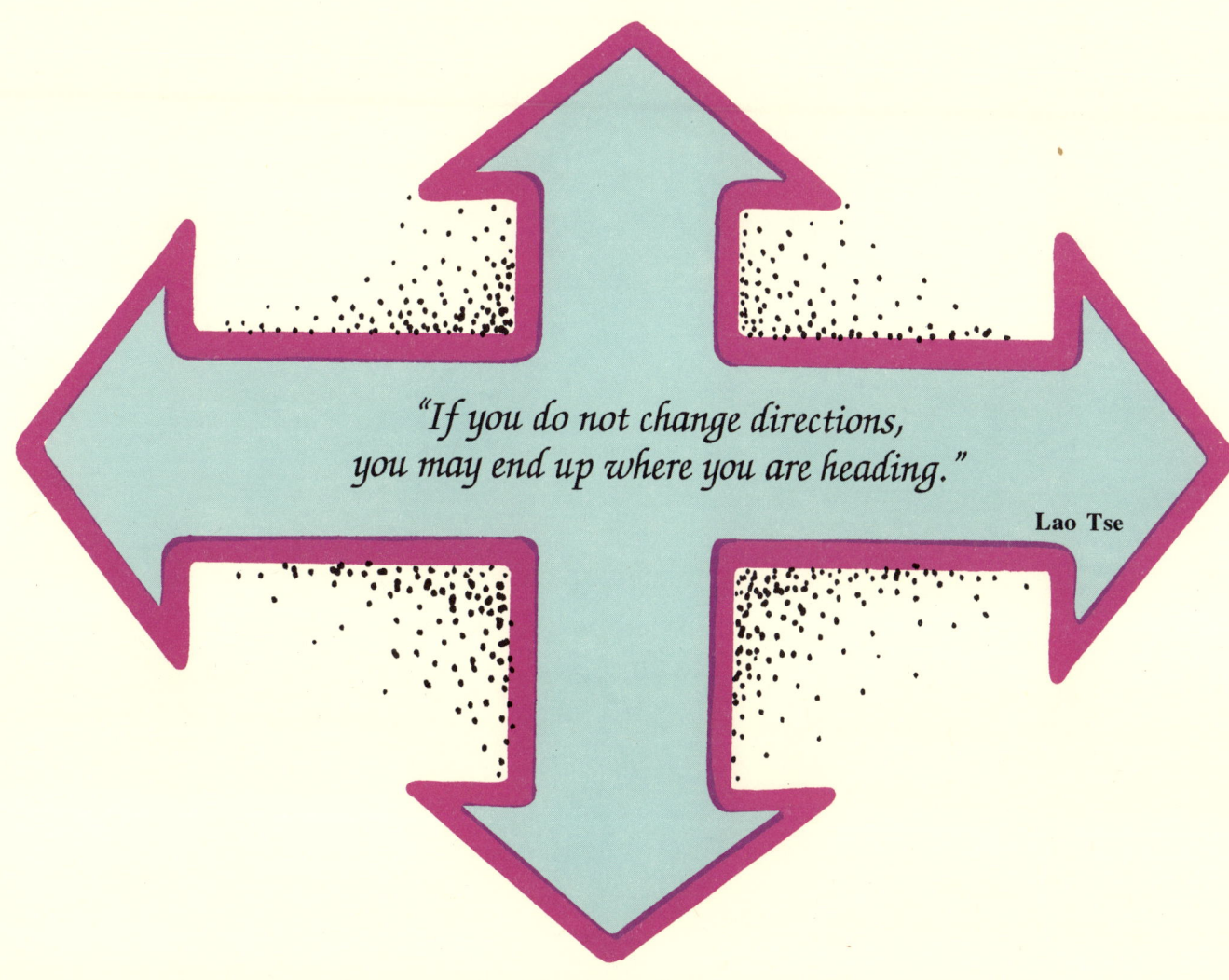

We are hurt people living in a hurtful world.

Are you hurting?
Is someone you love hurting?
Are you tired of living in the pain of the past?
Are you willing to do something about it?

Important hurts don't go away on their own.

You can choose to harbor hurt and resentment

or

you can choose to heal.

**You can recreate your life,
rebuild your self-esteem
and find inner peace.**

"We either make ourselves miserable or we make ourselves strong. The amount of work is the same."

Don Juan, Journey to Xtlan

The power of forgiveness is far greater than any tool or weapon known to man.[2] When you refuse to water a weed, it will die.

"When we heal our relationships, we heal ourselves."
Alan Cohen

We create our own worlds.

Yes, we were hurt.   Yes, it was wrong.

But now . . .

    it is our own responses to what happened that continue to hurt us.

Pogo said, "We have discovered the enemy and he is us."

Forgiveness begins with us.

You know who and what you need to forgive because of the pain and turmoil you feel when you think of them and their actions.

Let's examine ourselves honestly.

- ✓ How do you react when someone hurts you? Do you plan revenge? Do you go for the jugular?

- ✓ Do you want to keep telling them how much they hurt you and how? Do you want them to feel your pain?

- ✓ Do you feel events in your past have tainted your present?

- ✓ Are your relations with some people strained? Do you avoid speaking with or seeing them?

- ✓ Do your actions replay bad behavior you saw and hated as a child?

- ✓ Do you feel empty inside and try to fill the gap with substances?

- ✓ Do you keep getting in the same bad situation with person after person?

- ✓ Are you afraid of being hurt, afraid of failure, afraid of rejection, afraid to risk, always looking for a fight?

- ✓ Is your self-esteem suffering? Do you feel unhappy and unworthy?

There are other ways we may react when we've been hurt:

Silence　　　　　　Guilt　　　　　　　　Power plays　　　　　　　　Being a good guy
Withdrawal　　　　　　　　　　　Tears　　　　　　　　　　　　　　　　Insincerity
　　　　　　　Illusions – "If it hadn't happened, my life would be perfect"
Pretending we're "together"　　　　　　　　　　　　　　　　Inability to feel.

Though we try lots of ways to cover our pain, it becomes obvious.

WE HAVE NOT LET GO OF THE PAIN and IT HAS NOT LET GO OF US.[3]
NO MATTER HOW MUCH WE COVER IT, WE STILL FEEL THE BURN.

We deny and bury it by excessive behaviors:
drinking, eating, overworking, sex, drugs, spending, self-pity, endless TV watching, co-dependency, perfection.

We put on a happy face and deceive ourselves. We deny with words to minimize our pain. "It doesn't bother me. I'm not hurt. I'm not angry. I'm O.K. There are no problems here. Worse things have happened to others. It's not worth dredging up."

We become negative and bitter. Our relationships suffer. We have trouble at work. We abuse others and ourselves. We are depressed, hypersensitive, argumentative, self-righteous and distracted. Our energy is sapped. Our focus is narrow. We build walls and then feel lonely. We are critical of others because then we don't have to look at ourselves. We stay in the rut. Our life does not improve. We don't solve problems. We stay in the pain.

Our body is strongly affected physically by not forgiving. It's more visible than we think. Common physical results are stress, elevated blood pressure, increased stomach acidity, colitis, ulcers, arthritis, backaches, chest pains, migraines, anxiety attacks, and, even, cancer.

No matter what we say or think, our bodies tell the truth. They never lie.

It's not what you're eating that will get you.
It's what's eating you.

You never planned on nursing your wounds until they ruined your todays and dampened your tomorrows, but that may be what has occurred.

When you were hurt, you reacted the best you could, but the old behaviors that once helped you survive, now no longer serve you.

>We keep ourselves in the victim role when we don't change what we can.

Our reaction to resentment becomes

HABIT.

Like addictions,
we pass these habits on from generation to generation
until we deal with them.

We must deal with them now!

**The buck CAN stop here.
We CAN break the cycle**

for ourselves,   for our children   and for their children.

It is a miracle waiting to happen. It is in our hands.

We must be gentle with ourselves,

accept that we have made mistakes and realize we have punished ourselves long enough.

We need not be a victim anymore.
We can begin from where we are right now and
                                          walk the path of forgiveness and healing.

Once we decide to make the journey of forgiveness some things become apparent.

We will have to change.
We will have to learn how to react in new ways.
We do not know how to do this.
We are not sure how we'll feel or who we'll be if we change and let go.
We can't imagine our life without the pain.
We have come to know it and, even though it hurts and damages us, it fills us.
We fear the void and the unknown.

Forgiveness seems unfair.

But . . .

We can't make everything right - but - we can stop old wrongs from ruining our present and future.

Sometimes it feels good to be mad, to wallow in it self-righteously.

But it only feels good for awhile.

When we feed our victim role and focus on old pain, memories throb beneath our scars. Often, the hurter doesn't know, care or feel that we're hurting.

At a class on forgiveness the leader asked if someone would share a resentment with the group. I whipped my righteous hand in the air. I had a good one.

As I shared my seven year resentment of a friend, it was obvious. The group was all on my side. They agreed that I had been wronged and that I was the good guy.

Then the leader asked me a rude question. "WHY HAVEN'T YOU FORGIVEN HER?"

I was stunned. Speechless. I had NEVER thought of that. I didn't know what to say.

Then I mumbled bitterly, "Because if I forgive her, then she'll get away with it."

"Maureen, she got away with it seven years ago. She's out there living her life. She doesn't even know you're still hurting. So who are you really hurting by carrying this revenge around every day for seven years?"

It was obvious. She had made her point and I didn't like it. I was supposed to be the good guy. I didn't like feeling like a lunk in front of the group, even though I knew she was right.

I had been victimizing myself for the past seven years. My friend had hurt me once. Her actions may have been very cruel, wrong, and painful, but she was going on with her life while I was fueling the old hurt. I was trying to punish her by keeping the fire lit. Whenever I thought of her or what she had done, my mental VCR rewound and replayed the hurt over and over. Each time, it grew more vivid.

The leader asked me to wear a backpack full of bricks for the rest of the day. This was to help me feel and visualize the garbage I carried around inside each day and the heaviness of my burden.

So what was my immediate response? I resented the leader too.

We must heal these infected wounds so we can get on with our lives. To do this we need to focus on other parts of our lives -

love, laughter, growth, fun, adventure.

Negative attracts negative.

Positive attracts positive.

They are both cycles.
They are both our choices.

Often, the hardest person to forgive is yourself. This requires honesty.

Maybe you feel guilty for something you did.
Maybe you feel guilty for something you didn't do.

You must be specific as you forgive yourself. It may help to write down exactly what you haven't forgiven yourself for.

It is vital that we accept our past realistically, all of it, the good and the bad.

"The truth will set us free."
Jesus

You can't forgive what you don't accept.
                                                       You can't let go of what you don't forgive.

We can't go back and redo our life.
                                                  We can't change it to what we wish it had been.

We must accept it at face value,
    even the parts we ache over
     even the parts we can barely acknowledge
    even the parts we want to forget forever.

We need to realize that no matter what our past has been, our future is spotless.

There are others who are difficult to forgive.

Some are still mean and nasty to us.

Some are never sorry. They hurt us in awful ways and then leave us to deal with our deep wounds.

We want them to beg for our forgiveness but they don't.

We want them to pay, to hurt as we have.

Why don't they repent?

Their hearts may be so hard, they can no longer see wrong.

They may think they were right, that we deserved it.

They may not know they've harmed us.

They may be afraid to apologize.

They may be dead, leaving us with the burden.

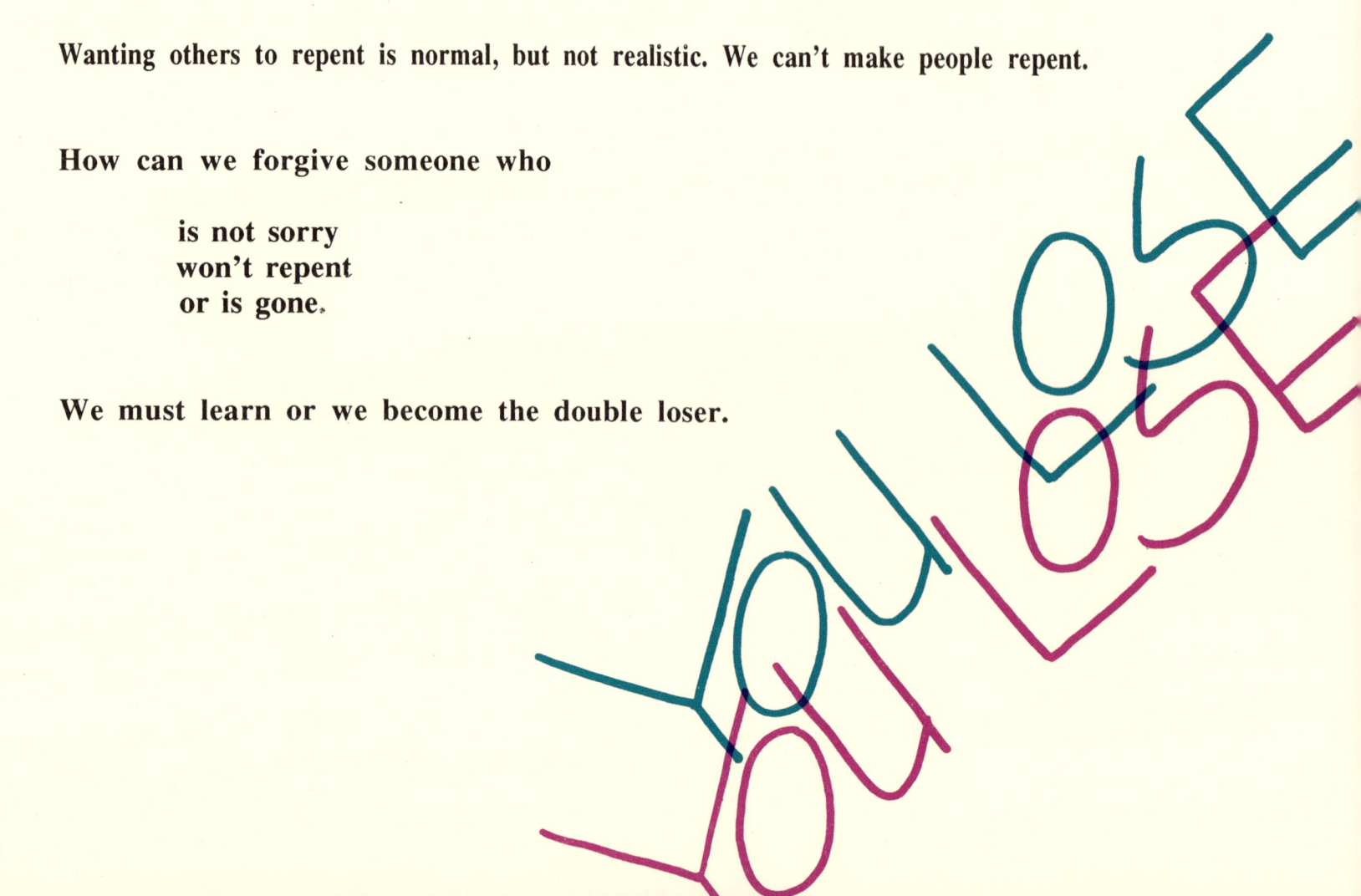

Wanting others to repent is normal, but not realistic. We can't make people repent.

How can we forgive someone who

>   is not sorry
>   won't repent
>   or is gone.

We must learn or we become the double loser.

The important thing is this.

We don't need their repentance to forgive.

Their repentance doesn't control us. We don't need it to heal and go on with our lives. We can walk the healing journey alone and be healed.

        Forgiveness is a process. It starts with a decision.

> **We choose to be
> grateful or ungrateful
> happy or miserable
> positive or negative
> forgiving or unforgiving.**

No one can make you forgive.

You choose to do it,

                and when you do,

                              you do it all for you.

B

*resentment
hate
anger*

Rarely have I met a person who isn't holding onto some resentment. Even the kindest, sweetest, most decent people I know - when asked if they resented anyone, spewed out bitter angry stories of how they or their loved ones had been wronged. I was shocked. I had thought I was a lesser person because I held resentments. Instead I discovered it is a part of our humanness. Resenting is a universal condition unless it is tempered with forgiveness.

Resentments are things you've held on to, lived with and never forgiven. They imprison you.

They work like a revolving door,
the same ole'   same ole'

                        Here it comes again . . . . .
                        Here it comes again . . . . .
                        Here it comes again . . . . .
                        Here it comes again . . . . .

            and we rehurt every time it comes.

Some resentments are hidden, and because there's a destructive power in keeping them secret, we must let them out and deal with them.

The worst kind of resentment is where everyone sympathizes with you.

"Oh, you poor thing. They were SO mean! And you were SO good."

Such resentments may feel soothing. Martyrdom seems righteous. But being hurt does not make you a saint. In reality, these resentments fester and fester and eat up your energy.

**Hate is a deeper dimension of resentment. Like cocaine, it seems to give us a high, to feel good. With it comes a feeling of power and righteousness.
This is an illusion.**

Hate, like acid, will damage the vessel in which it is stored as well as the object on which it is poured.

Hate is addictive. It may be our hardest habit to break. We will have to break it over and over before it finally leaves.

Is there a difference between hate and anger?

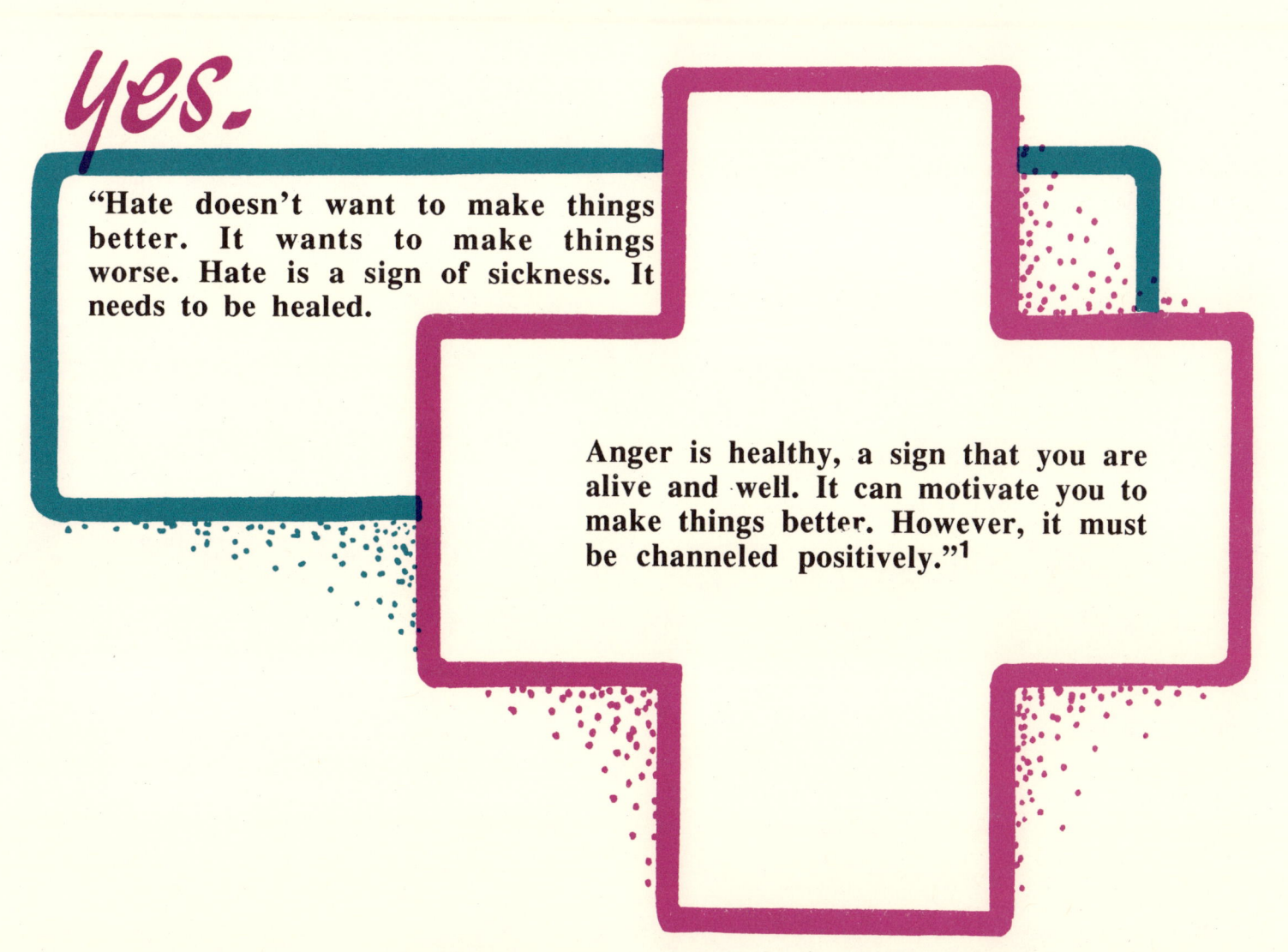

yes.

"Hate doesn't want to make things better. It wants to make things worse. Hate is a sign of sickness. It needs to be healed.

Anger is healthy, a sign that you are alive and well. It can motivate you to make things better. However, it must be channeled positively."[1]

Anger is a valid feeling. It is necessary for good mental health. It isn't good or bad. It just is.

We need to get angry over the injustices done to us.

We cannot forgive, heal or let go of our pain until we let the anger out. The flipside of anger is helplessness.

Do you

↪ not "do" anger?

↪ not feel you have any anger to get in touch with?

↪ not recognize anger when you feel it?

"I don't get angry. I just get hurt."

That was my motto for 42 years. I believed it. I nurtured it. My anger was buried so deeply and always hidden so quickly that I did not realize it was there.

I played this game until the death of someone who had hurt me deeply when I was a child. At first I noticed I had no grief over the death. Then I felt guilt over that. But still no anger surfaced.

Then, slowly, it bubbled up, like a poisonous gas, unable to be contained by my personal facade. It showed itself in tears and sobs as I would be driving alone, uncalled for, not understood. Why was I crying for no reason? My life was so good. I was so happy. La-de-da.

Close friends and family worried. I saw a counselor about an unrelated issue. The emotional dam burst.

Anger at years of abuse, injustices, betrayals, neglect and prejudice erupted. I cried more. I hurt more. "This is stupid," I sobbed to my mate. "I'm 40 years old. Why am I crying over my childhood? It's over."

He gently urged me to stay with the process, "to get it out until it is gone." I didn't want to, but I did.

Indirect expressions of anger are common to people who feel they don't "do" anger. You can feel innocent when people you are angry at lose their cool, which is just what you were hoping for.

Indirect expressions of anger are -

| lateness | gossip | ignoring | silence | brooding | teasing |

| forgetting | ignoring | embarrassing | sarcasm | avoiding eyes |

looking through them   phony smiles and looks   put down humor

banging things unnecessarily   violence   breaking, soiling or losing their things

substance abuse   anger at other things - minor issues, driving, objects.

Anger is at the core of our resentments. It has to be expressed or it stays in the body. Many of us have never learned how to express anger positively. We associate anger with rage, violence and abuse. We must relearn.

Anger isn't bad, expressing it negatively is.

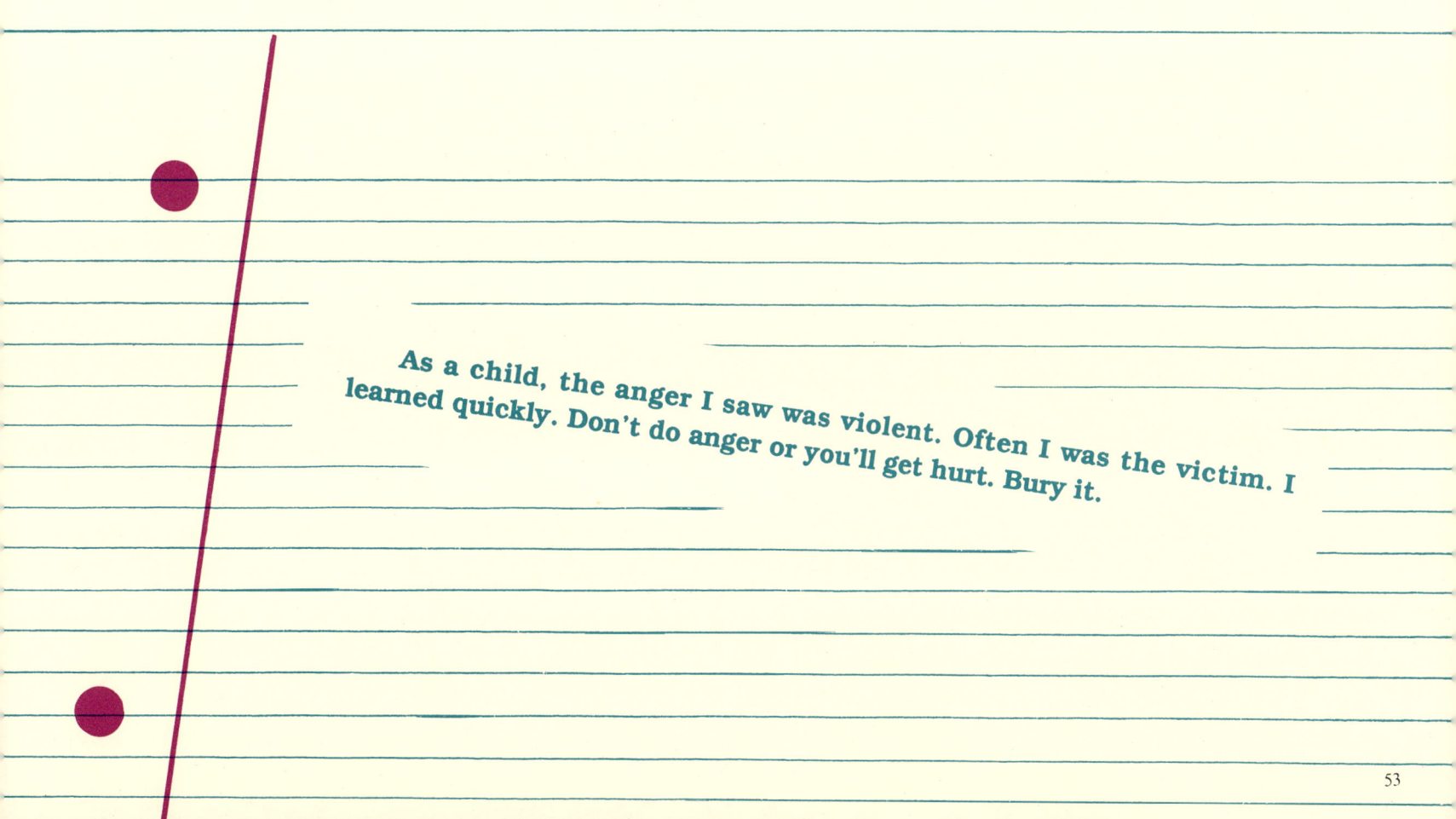

As a child, the anger I saw was violent. Often I was the victim. I learned quickly. Don't do anger or you'll get hurt. Bury it.

Negative expressions of anger do not solve problems or heal. When you do them, your anger, not you, is in charge. Rage consumes you as it steals your time, energy and joy.

Do you express your anger

                                positively or negatively?

Expressions of negative anger are -

hitting
verbal abuse
making threats
swearing
demanding
breaking things
throwing things
slamming doors
hanging up the phone
name calling
put downs
spanking
kicking
shouting
driving recklessly
pounding fists
blowing off steam in a negative way
verbally going for the person's sore spots
dumping your grievances in someone's lap without staying around to talk it out
withdrawal of acceptance and love.

Releasing anger healthily is simply thinking about what you will do before you do it and choosing a positive outlet, rather than unleashing it negatively and then thinking how you did it wrong.

respond----

It is responding rather than reacting.

REACT

Some positive ways to express anger are:

walking	running	biking	exercise	showers

gardening	talking to others	punching pillows or punching bags

stomping	crying	playing with a pet or person	dancing

counseling	vacuuming	cleaning	hot baths	massage

singing	relaxation exercises	meditation	screaming in a solitary place

throwing balls or darts	praying	hitting tennis or golf balls	writing in a journal

writing a letter you don't send	beating plastic bats on beds	talking to a third party

confronting the person directly - honestly, straight forwardly.

Anger must be expressed or it stays in our body and pollutes our beings.

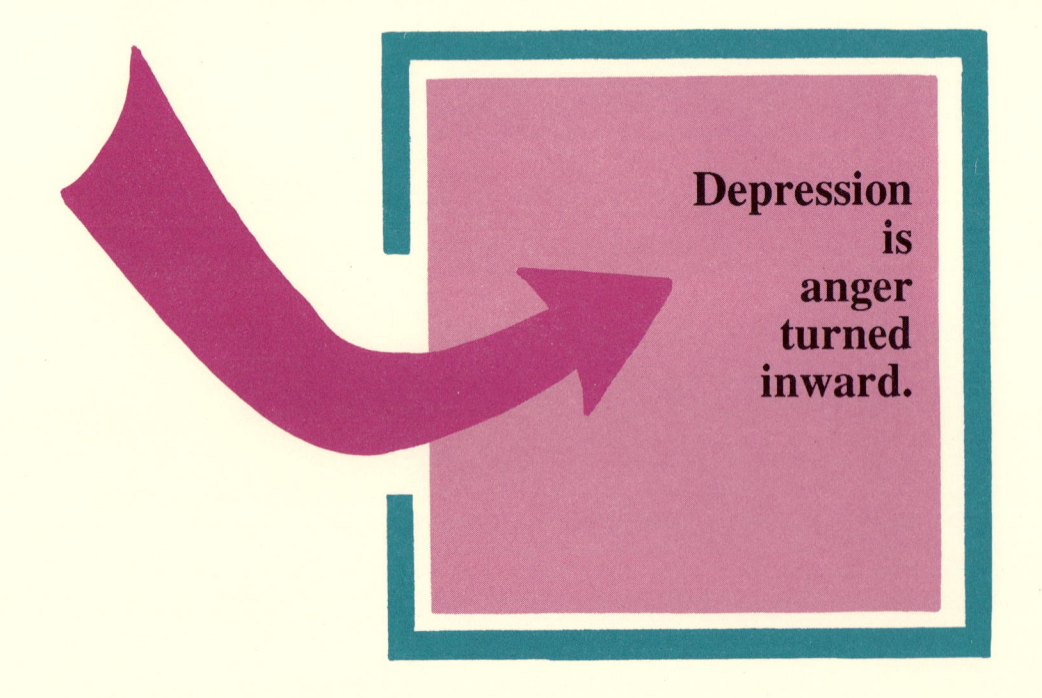

Depression is anger turned inward.

"When you bury your feelings, you bury them alive."
John Powell

Anger hides other feelings -

fear   guilt   hurt   grief   shame   embarrassment

frustration   distrust   powerlessness   loneliness   inadequacy.

When we finally vent our anger, that is still not enough. We must dig deeper and unearth the rest of our buried feelings. Only then do we begin to heal the wounds.

Why do we cling to our resentments, hate and anger so stubbornly?

Holding on protects us in some ways. It keeps us at a distance and makes us less vulnerable.

Once we let it go, we have to deal with and feel our pain.

Usually we want two things -

       to keep our anger,

       to have peace.

This is not possible. We cannot have both. We must make a choice. What we are talking about here is cancelling the debt.

       What do you want to have -

          anger and resentment

            or

          peace and healing?

       The word forgive means to give up.

Beneath all anger and resentment is a demand.

They didn't do it our way.

We wanted this.   We got that.

We can want others to do things our way, but we can't demand it. Being angry for years because we didn't get what we wanted is destructive.

I wanted storybook parents. I didn't get them.

Now I realize I need to accept them for what they were and are. They had their own painful history and parental examples. They did the best they could. They didn't get up in the morning and say, "Let's hurt the kids today!"

They tried to be a good family. They loved us. They did many good things. As I unleash my anger and bad memories, I can also see the good ones, and I can love them in an honest and realistic way.

John Bradshaw says,
"I wanted my Dad to be a tall oak tree, but he was just a bush."

We can apply this insight to anyone who hurt us, not just parents. We wanted those who hurt us to be more than they were, or could be, at that particular time.

We must accept the imperfections of others and ourselves. None of us is perfect.

The most painful thing my counselor ever said to me was, "You need to say good-by to the parents you never had. You can't get peaches off an acorn tree."

When I was able to stop crying, I began to see that I had put them on pedestals. I wanted them there. I needed them there to survive in my fantasy world and I had perpetuated my fantasy because, as a child, the reality was not bearable. I had used this tool to survive and it had worked, but now it no longer served me. Now I needed to face reality, accept it, heal and move on. In essence, I needed to forgive.

When we get to the healing, we accept them just as they are, even in their weaknesses and human failings.

It is not our place to demand perfection of them.

What they did was not right, but they are more than their bad actions

and so are we.

4 who & what do we need to forgive

Our lives are shaped by those who love us and those who won't.

Even though it may not have been intentional, many people in our lives have hurt us deeply and unfairly.

It might have been

mates lovers siblings parents systems ourselves friends children

professional co-horts others.

strangers counselors employers

churches grandparents teachers clergy relatives childhood peers

How do we know what to forgive?

We don't need to forgive petty irritations. They are just part of life. What we do need to forgive are deep, personal hurts.

                                          Hurts that are unfair, undeserved.

We need to forgive actions or deeds, not qualities.

We need to forgive them

                        for doing something
                     not for being something

                 for what they did or did not do
                 not for who or what they were

                            for verbs
                    not for adjectives or nouns

                   for behaviors and actions
                      not for the person.

Lewis Smedes says,

"If you are still harboring resentments toward your parents, you will need to work on those first. As long as we resent our parents, we never grow up. The stuff of families is bloodier and more passionate. The wounds are deeper and hardest to heal. The blood clot has to be cleared."

Why is this true?

When we are hurt as children, it threatens our very survival, our trust, safety, security and self-esteem.

It affects how we look at ourselves, other people and our relationships. It comes at a time when we are forming our attitudes, beliefs and behaviors. Our entire life foundation is distorted and damaged.

IS IT TIME FOR YOU TO FORGIVE YOUR PARENTS

OR

DO YOU WANT TO PUT IT OFF A BIT LONGER?[1]

As a five year old child, I knew that my parents' behavior was wrong. I reported the abuse and when I wasn't believed or protected, I suffered a double betrayal, once from the abuser and once from the enabler.

A child does not know where else to go or what else to do. So we do the best we can. We absolve them and go on. We focus on the positive. We do what we need to do to survive.

Perhaps you are still nursing childhood hurts yet not sure if you were abused. Abuse can be -

1. Physical -

> Being hit, whipped, beaten, bitten, pushed, burned. This may or may not have caused visible marks such as bruises, burns, welts, scratches, broken bones or hemorrhaging. Physical discipline can become abuse when it includes excessive spanking, kicking or whipping, resulting in injuries. Using a fist or instrument to hit or hitting vulnerable places like the face, stomach, back or genitals can be abusive. Punishment can also be abusive when it is extreme and inappropriate to the child's age and ability to understand.

2. Sexual -

> When you are forced, tricked, threatened or coerced into any kind of sexual contact. This includes inappropriate touching, sexual intercourse, showing pornographic things to children or taking sexual pictures of them or talking to them about explicit sexual things.

3. Verbal/Emotional -

> When a child is psychologically badgered, belittled, lied to, threatened, or constantly called negative names.

4. Neglect -

> When a parent doesn't provide basic necessities such as medical, dental and hygienic attention, clothing, food, shelter or protection. It also occurs when a child is left alone without proper care or when the parent is not emotionally or physically available to the child. Failing to talk, hold, or hug a child is neglect.

Perhaps you weren't abused but need to forgive a spouse or parents who are or were

overbearing
unaffectionate
absent
distant
overprotective
belittling
held you back
put you down
expected too much or not enough
non-nurturing

As part of our healing process, it is important to understand the abuser's behavior and weaknesses.

But no matter what the problems were, there are no reasons for abusing a child or adult.

Perhaps you need to forgive other things in your life -

broken marriages   broken families   broken relationships   disappointment   deception

infidelity   humiliation   betrayal   jealousy   rejection   ridicule

gossip   abandonment   discrimination   prejudice   insensitivity

being hurt because of your -

race   religion   disabilities   looks   poverty

ideas   feelings   successes   failures   gender

being -

belittled   berated   labeled   taunted   teased   hurt   misjudged.

5

what forgiveness is & is not

FORGIVENESS IS NOT FORGETTING

There are some things we should never forget or we invite them to repeat themselves.

Forgiveness heals our memories but it doesn't erase them. We don't get amnesia when we forgive. The memories will remain, fading in and out with clarity. The pain will subside and become bearable.

Can we remember and still forgive?   *yes*

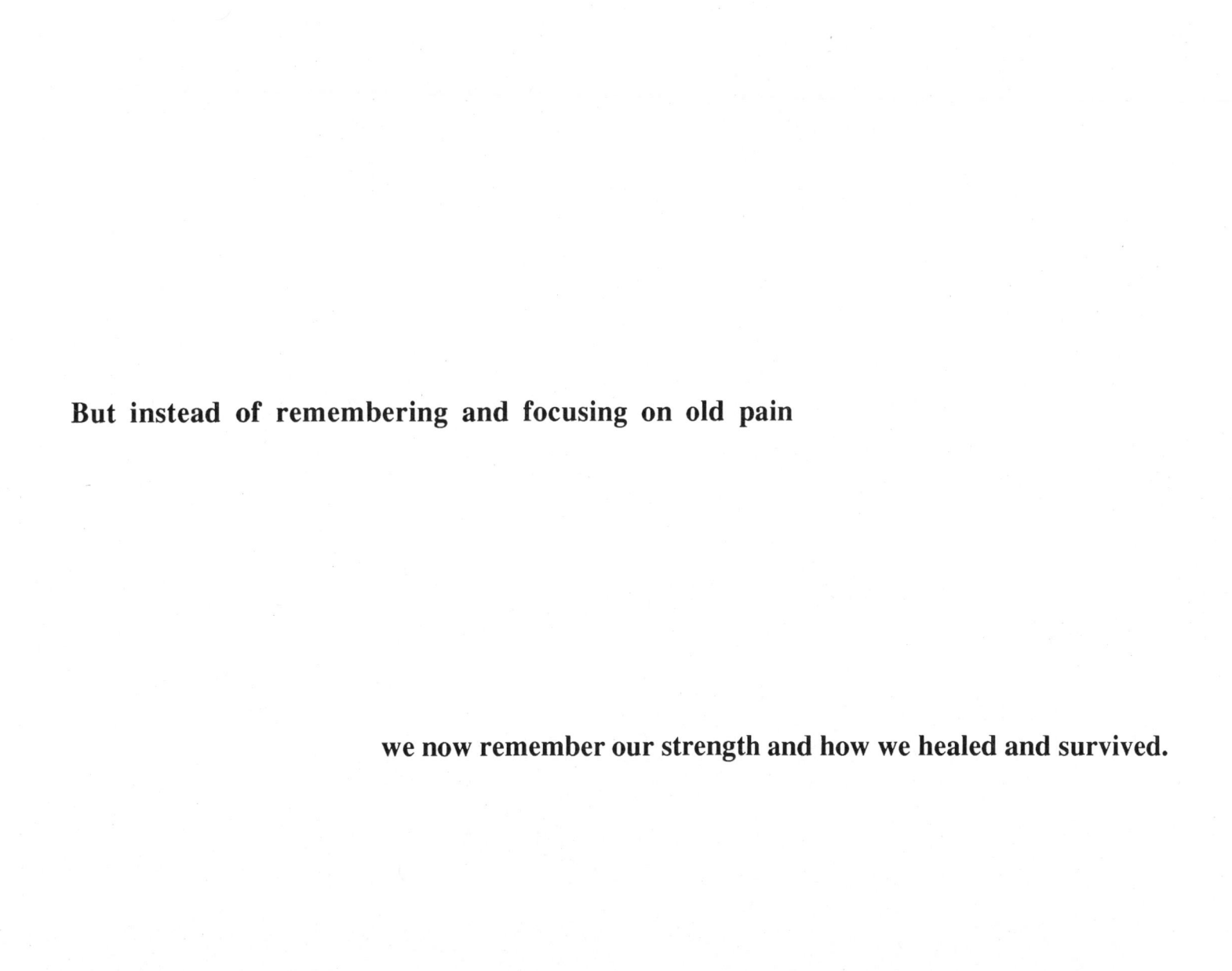

But instead of remembering and focusing on old pain

we now remember our strength and how we healed and survived.

FORGIVENESS IS NOT HAVING TO UNDERSTAND EVERYTHING.

Accept confusion as you forgive. Too much talk can get in the way. Don't try to figure out exactly who did or said what, when, where and why. Don't wait for blame to be settled and agreed upon.

Complete understanding and agreement is too much to ask in the beginning. However it may come later, a piece at a time.

FORGIVENESS IS NOT TRUSTING.

"Trust is built on evidence.

Some people should never be trusted and to trust them again is crazy. We don't have to become fools to become forgivers."

Lewis Smedes

FORGIVENESS IS NOT GIVING UP OR GIVING IN.

FORGIVENESS IS NOT ABSOLUTION.

They remain responsible for what they did, but only they can make peace with their own past. Our forgiveness does not let them off the hook.

FORGIVENESS IS NOT TOLERATING, EXCUSING OR CONDONING.

When we forgive we are not saying the behavior was acceptable nor are we saying we will allow it to happen again.

FORGIVENESS IS NOT SUPPRESSING CONFLICT.

Pacifying and keeping things quiet denies feelings and robs yourself and others of the experience of forgiveness.

FORGIVENESS CAN'T BE FORCED OR PHONY.

We can't forgive because it's our duty or because someone says we should.

Forgiveness must come honestly and from the heart.

A man convinced against his will is of the same opinion still.

Beware of indifferent forgiveness.

> "Oh, that's O.K. No problem."

This is usually denial, not forgiveness. Denial becomes a habit and can be as comfortable as an old shoe.

DON'T FORGIVE TOO FAST.

Be patient. Forgiveness takes time. It can't be rushed. It comes in steps, a little at a time. The deeper the wound the longer it takes to forgive.

Rapid forgiveness may be denial rather than healing. You may be trying to control or manipulate rather than letting go.

DON'T WAIT FOR OTHERS TO REPENT.

They may never.

DON'T WAIT TO GET EVEN TO FORGIVE.

You never will.

When we forgive, we surrender our right to resent.

We wish them well.
We let go.
We heal.

FORGIVENESS CAN BE SILENT AND WITHIN.

You don't always have to tell them you forgive them. Your actions and behavior can show it.

When I forgave her she never knew. Neither had she known I was angry with her for seven years. I was always nice to her face. Then I'd go home and restab myself emotionally as I'd mentally replay the painful memories of her actions. When I forgave her, I did not forget what she had done, but it no longer hurt when I remembered. My resentment and anger had been internal and so was my forgiveness.

When he was dying I sent him flowers. I didn't do it for him; I did it for me. I did not write a note. I did not say I forgive you. I did not say, "Hey, no problem, it was O.K." I just signed my name. He knew his actions and he had to face them on his own. I didn't need his repentance to forgive and get my peace and healing.

DO NOT WAIT FOR CIRCUMSTANCES TO BE RIGHT TO FORGIVE.

They may never be right.

REALIZE THERE WILL BE PAIN IN THE PROCESS.

Your pain needs to run its course. We feel uncomfortable with emotional pain because we've been raised only to express our physical pain.

IS THERE ANGER AFTER FORGIVING?

Yes. It's natural.

Anger and forgiveness can live together in the same heart.[1] Just because you sometimes feel anger when you remember, does not mean you haven't forgiven.

It is wonderful if anger dissolves as you forgive, but expecting it to, is not realistic.

ANGER *forgiveness*

ACCEPT IMPERFECT FORGIVING.

We don't do anything else perfectly; probably we won't forgive perfectly either.

Perfection holds us back and keeps us from doing what we need to do.

LIMIT YOUR EXPECTATIONS OF FORGIVENESS.

You may never get a rosy ending.

You may never be best friends again.

You may never kiss and make up.

You may never like them again.

You may have to let them go out of your life.

3 steps to forgiveness

1. The Act

2. The Process

3. The State

When I decided I needed to forgive and realized I didn't know how, I went to a spiritual adviser. She explained three steps and then she prayed with me. I didn't want to forgive. I did it through clenched teeth. My head told me I should. My emotions wanted to hold on to my resentments.

God grant me the serenity to accept the things I cannot change, the courage to change the things I can and the wisdom to know the difference.

Serenity Prayer

Alexander Pope said, "To err is human, to forgive divine." I agree. I believe forgiveness is not a human thing. I think it is a God thing. My humanness doesn't tell me to forgive. It tells me to get even. I probably won't. I'm too nice a person, but I'll want to and I'll fantasize about it.

I also do not believe I can overcome my resentments and pain just because I decide to or because someone else tells me I should. I believe it only happens when I bring God in to do the job with me. I believe forgiveness is a grace from God, a gift that we can receive upon the asking, but one that we WORK very very hard to obtain.

Step 1 - The Act

We choose to forgive them and heal, even though it still hurts and even though we may still feel angry and want to get even.

After we decide to forgive, our emotions will get in line. It will take time but it will happen.

When we make a decision to let it go, we don't have to like it but we do have to be sincere.

Let Go and Let God

As children bring their broken toys with tears for us to mend,
 I brought my broken dreams to God, because He was my friend.

But then, instead of leaving Him in peace to work alone, I hung around and tried to help with ways that were my own.

At last I snatched them back and cried, "How can you be so slow?"

"My child," He said, "What could I do? You never did let go."

Unknown

**Grace is the sense that
God actually does get into us and work through us.**

If we ask and are still, he can perform the miracle of healing the hurts we never deserved and fill the spaces within us with peace and forgiveness.

Pray for the person you need to forgive, perhaps even out loud. You can do it through clenched teeth. You don't have to like doing it. You just have to mean it. It's like priming a pump. It opens you to God's power and allows Him to perform His miracle and free you of the hate, resentment, anger and pain.

"If you have a resentment you want to be free of, if you will pray for the person or the thing you resent, you will be free. If you will ask in prayer for everything you want for yourself to be given to them, you will be free. Ask for their health, their prosperity, their happiness, and you will be free. Even when you don't really want it for them, and your prayers are only words and you don't mean it, go ahead and do it anyway. Do it every day for two weeks and you will find you have come to mean it and want it for them, and you will realize that where you used to feel bitterness and resentment and hatred, you now feel compassionate understanding and love."

The Big Book, Alcoholics Anonymous

Pray . . .

_____, I bless you and wish you well. I release you to your highest good.

We can forgive in many ways -

★face to face

★by letter

★by phone

★by actions

★silently

★alone

★within ourselves

I confronted her face to face and asked her why she hadn't protected me. She told me what it had been like for her, how she hadn't known what to do, how she had felt she had no options. As she talked, a healing took place. I could feel the resentment and anger drain out of me physically. Tears cleansed my pain and memories, leaving me remembering, but now understanding and healed. Honest forgiveness filled me and remains to this day.

I confronted him in a letter. I used 'I' statements. "I feel _____. I don't understand _____." I closed it, "I want our relationship to improve. I want to understand. I want to have you in my life. I am open to talking, if you are."

Before I sent the letter, I discussed it with a counselor. We examined the wording, the message. We went over all the possible results. What if I never heard from him again? What if he died before we talked it out? What if he thought I was all wrong and attacked me?

The counselor asked me if I could live with all the options.

"Yes."

"Then send it."

Before I did, I prayed and asked God to intercede and bless this communication and healing.

Upon receiving my letter, he called me immediately. We met and talked. Although he had been aware of my distance and, often, my sarcasm, he was surprised by my feelings.

As we talked honestly, we cried. Again, healing and understanding came and pain left.

Forgiveness left me feeling healed and able to accept him as imperfect yet doing the best he could and honestly loving me along the way.

Our offenders and abusers were also victims. There are good and bad sides to everyone. Can you see this in those who have hurt you?

There were twin boys. One was an optimist, always finding joy. The other was a pessimist, always finding negative.

Hoping to blend their attitudes, their parents came up with an idea. For their birthday, they gave the pessimist a room full of wonderful toys. When he saw them, he cried, "Is this all I get?"

They gave the optimist a room full of pony poop. Upon seeing it, he squealed happily, "You can't fool me! With all this poop, there's got to be a pony in here someplace!"

It's important for us to find our pony.

When we walk through the pain,
gifts wait on the other side.

What have you learned and become
because of the pain you suffered?

What good qualities and strengths have you developed?

BE PROUD OF THESE.

Step 2 - The Process

We let the feelings and memories process.

There is no timetable. Because our hurts are unique, each of us has to heal in a unique way.

The only way out of pain is through it. We need to feel and express our grief, hurt and anger.

We need to mourn, feel the sadness and pain.

*"Tears won't bring him back,
but they might bring you back."*
Barbra Streisand in <u>Prince of Tides</u>

When we shove feelings under the carpet, they just come up and make ripples that we will trip on.[1]

WHAT YOU RESIST PERSISTS.

"The silence was worse than the rapes."
Barbra Streisand in <u>Prince of Tides</u>

Feelings aren't right or wrong. They are just the way we feel.

We are not responsible for our feelings. We are responsible for what we do with those feelings, the actions and behaviors we use to express them.

Step 3 - The State

You see them, you remember, but it doesn't hurt you.

You have let it go.

"We do not see things as they are, but as we are."
The Talmud

Comes the Dawn

With your head up and your eyes open
After a while you learn the subtle difference
Between holding a hand and chaining a soul,
And you learn that love doesn't mean security,
And you begin to learn that kisses aren't contracts
And presents aren't promises
And you begin to accept your defeats
With the grace of a woman, not the grief of a child,
And you learn to build all your roads
On today because tomorrow's ground
Is too uncertain. And futures have
A way of falling down in midflight.
After a while you learn that even sunshine burns if you get too much.
so you plant your own garden and decorate your own soul,
Instead of waiting for someone to bring you flowers.
And you learn that you really can endure . . .
That you really are strong,
And you really do have worth
And you learn and learn
With every good-bye you learn.

Anonymous

Forgiveness is not an event, it's a process.

Nobody said it would be easy and no one can make it easier for you.

Even when you feel it's not coming, don't give up.

Sometimes you struggle with it so long and then realize it is within you, that forgiveness happened and you didn't even realize when you finally did it.

You know it's happened, because the memories don't hurt when you remember them and you feel new empathy and understanding toward your offender.

As we accept the past for what it was, the bad and the good,

we must turn toward our future.

FUTURE

Forgiveness is a miracle
        but it isn't a miracle cure for all that ails you.

Do you need to make positive changes in your life -

        physically, intellectually, emotionally or spiritually?

Is it time to love yourself and not look for love in other, wrong places?

Things to stop or avoid -

criticizing   blaming   judging   feeling guilty

regretting   feeling shame   old negative habits and people

being with people who discourage your strengths and support your weaknesses.

Stop using what happened to you as an excuse for everything that's wrong with your life.

Good things we can do for ourselves to speed up our healing process -

talk to trustworthy people　　　　take walks　　　　nap　　　　meditate

be joyful　　　play　　　be spontaneous　　　cry　　　see a counselor

make positive healthy choices　　　　take time for yourself　　　　risk

buy a special gift to celebrate your growth　　　　enjoy music you love

join a support group　　　　learn　　　　apologize

hobbies　　　crafts　　　garden　　　write　　　listen to /see tapes

finish projects　　　　get productive　　　　attend classes

repair relationships　　　learn from your mistakes　　　stop addictions

put supportive people in your life as role models　　　keep a journal

exercise　　　　eat healthy　　　　eliminate self-defeating behaviors.

Place an attractive picture of yourself, as a child or an adult, in a special frame in a prominent spot. Each time you see it, say, "I love you. I think you're great. I take good care of you."

Get an empty book.

Each day fill a page like this:

+'s: List three positive things about yourself, the first things you think of today. Do more than three if you are on a roll.

Thank yous: List a paragraph of everything you are grateful for today. Write the first things that pop into your head.

Prayer requests: Fill the rest of the page with a list of concerns you want to give to God, whatever comes into your mind. Ask for what you want and need today. Ask God to bless your requests and for His will to be done.

1.

2.

3.

Thank yous:

Prayer requests:

Use Daily Affirmations:

From today on, I am in charge of my life.

Today I rise above my limitations.

Today I release all my hurts and resentments
and let forgiveness set me free.

Today I say yes to me and to love and to my power
to make positive decisions.

My past is over and can't be changed.
Today I accept it and let it go lovingly.

I am creating a happier life by practicing forgiveness
of myself and others.

Miracles are happening to me because I am willing
to be changed and healed.

I feel happy and free.

DO THIS EXERCISE.

Take a few minutes to clear your head and spirit of negativity.

Visualize a big trash can suspended from a huge balloon in the sky. Feel all your pain, hurts, resentments and bitterness. Mentally tie each one to a white balloon and watch it rise to the sky and into the trash can. When they are all in the can, put the lid on and let it drift out of sight. Let it go. Feel it go. Feel the lightness within you. This is space for you and God to fill with positive healing and forgiveness.

Be positive.

Realize that without the pain you would never have initiated the change.

"I would not have grown one bit if I had not learned to forgive."
Marie Balter

Go easy on yourself.

Forgiveness occurs one step at a time
and sometimes they are just baby steps.

what happens when we forgive

7

moving on ›››››

WE LEARN NEW WAYS.

Autobiography in Five Short Chapters

I.
I walk down the street.
There is a deep hole in the sidewalk.
I fall in.
I am lost . . . I am helpless . . . It isn't my fault.
It takes forever to find a way out.

II.
I walk down the same street.
There is a deep hole in the sidewalk.
I pretend I don't see it.
I fall in again.
I can't believe I am in the same place again, but it isn't my fault.
It still takes a long time to get out.

III.
I walk down the same street.
There is a deep hole in the sidewalk.
I see it there.
I still fall in . . . it's a habit.
My eyes are open . . . I know where I am . . . It is my fault.
I get out immediately.

IV.
I walk down the same street.
There is a deep hole in the sidewalk.
I walk around it.

V.
I walk down another street.

Portia Nelson

WE SEE A REVISION IN OUR VISION.

We see the person who hurt us through new eyes. Before we saw them as the bad person who hurt us. Later we see them in greater perspective, as a hurter who was flawed, weak, sick, needy, ignorant.

WE FEEL NEW FEELINGS.

The pain, rage and resentment fade away and do not stab at us when we remember. We reach a point where we don't have to stir it up anymore. We are now full of acceptance, freedom, compassion and peace. What happened no longer determines how we feel about ourselves or our future.

We are more than a victim.

I saw a movie that paralleled my story. Afterwards, I realized I had watched the entire film without pain. Before, if I saw a story similar to mine, I would sob uncontrollably, falling into a somber depression of pain and memories.

This was when I discovered I had been healed. I told my husband, "The counselor healed me. My pain is gone. I'm all better. He's wonderful."

My husband wisely said, "No, he didn't heal you. You did. Give yourself credit for all the hard work. He helped the process but you did it. Be proud of yourself."

I am.

As you heal, you will laugh again. You will laugh at life and yourself.

"The root of humor is not joy - it is pain."
Mark Twain

"A person without a sense of humor is like a wagon without springs, jilted by every possible pebble in the road."
Karen Kaiser Clark

"You grow up the day you have the first real laugh at yourself."
Ethel Barrymore

WE CHANGE WHAT WE CAN.

When we refuse to forgive we can't grow.

Now we grow.

Inner peace is created by changing yourself, not the people who hurt you.[1]

Do you have a vision for how you want to feel and what you want your future to be like?

Are you changing yourself for yourself?

"The greatest discovery in our generation is that human beings, by changing the inner attitudes of their minds, can change the outer aspects of their lives."
William James

"Oh, God, I ain't what I ought to be
and God, I ain't what I want to be
dear God, I ain't what I'm gonna be
but thank god I ain't what I used to be."

anonymous

WE BELIEVE WE CAN.

"Whether you say you can or whether you say you can't, you're right."

Henry Ford

Can you forgive?

You need to make a decision about what you want.

Do you want to keep suffering or do you want to heal?

Can you set yourself free?

There is only one thing that can prevent you from forgiving and that is your will, simply refusing to do it.

It is not "you would if you could."   You can.

It is in your hands.

Let go.

Lord,

*give me the guidance to know when to hold on
and when to let go*

and the grace to make the right decision with dignity.

WE SET NEW BOUNDARIES.

Freedom is strength and you get it when you use your power to forgive.

When you forgive, you show new respect for yourself.

When you respect yourself, you set new limits.

You no longer tolerate certain negative behaviors or abuse.

"I'm a survivor. Being a survivor doesn't mean you have to be made out of steel and it doesn't mean you have to be ruthless. It means you have to be basically on your own side."
                                               Linda Ronstadt

WE ACCEPT REALITY.

"To love at all is to be vulnerable. Love anything and your heart will certainly be wrung and possibly be broken. If you want to make sure of keeping it intact, you must give your heart to no one, not even to an animal. Wrap it carefully round with hobbies and little luxuries; avoid all entanglements; lock it up safe in the casket or coffin of your selfishness . . . it will not be broken; it will become unbreakable, impenetrable, irredeemable. The only place outside Heaven where you can be perfectly safe from the dangers of love is Hell!"

C. S. Lewis

We have to face the reality of living in an imperfect world.

We will be hurt again, but now we know new truths.

Pain is inevitable.

Suffering is optional.

WE MOVE ON.

Your healing, just like your pain, is unique to you. We've all been hurt by different people in a variety of ways. We've all reacted in our own styles. We are all at different stages in our physical and emotional adulthood. We all have different external and internal resources available to help us heal.

But healing is an option for each of us, if we choose it and are willing to pay the price. The price is facing the pain, letting go, acceptance and growth.

Don't get discouraged if forgiveness seems difficult for you. It is difficult for everyone at first.

When you see a man on the top of a mountain,

you can bet he didn't fall there.

The journey of 1000 miles begins with a single step.
Lao Tzu

Take it.

Forgiveness is a gift you give yourself.

PUBLICATIONS AVAILABLE BY MAUREEN BURNS

Run With Your Dreams (Book) $10.00

    A motivation capsule on how to get what you want out of your gift of life. With an easy format, it is a book for any adult with dreams.

Corre Con Tus Sueños (Book) $10.00

    Spanish Version of Run With Your Dreams

Poursuis Tes Reves (Book) $10.00

    French Version of Run With Your Dreams

Getting In Touch/Intimacy (Book) $10.00

    A book with an easy format. Practical ways to enrich the many relationships in your life both with others and with yourself.

Forgiveness/A Gift You Give Yourself (Book) $15.00

    An invaluable tool for forgiving others and forgiving oneself. Simple, direct, from-the-heart.

Cara's Story (Book) $10.00

    For children. Written with her daughter, Cara. It is a true story told through the eyes of a child and deals with death, loss, caring and hope.

Run With Your Dreams (Audio Cassette) $10.00

    A 60 minute live presentation on motivation by Maureen Burns, " . . . witty, touching and dynamic!"

Forgiveness (Audio Cassette) $10.00

    A 60 minute live presentation on forgiveness by Maureen Burns, " . . . from-the-heart insights that could change your life!"

Maureen Burns on Humor (Audio Cassette) $10.00

    A 60 minute live presentation on humor by Maureen Burns, "This tape should be bottled, capped and prescribed!"

Change Happens (Audio Cassette) $10.00

    A 75 minute live presentation on coping with change by Maureen Burns, extremely enjoyable and educational.

To order, send a check payable to:
Empey Enterprises, 810 Alexander Street, Greenville, Michigan 48838
(616) 754-7036   Fax (616) 754-8122
e-mail: maureenb@pathwaynet.com

Include your name, address, phone, number of books and title(s) you want.
Please add $3.50 shipping for first item ordered and .50¢ for each additional item.
For Visa and MasterCard orders please call (616) 754-7036.
For large quantity discounts contact Empey Enterprises.

NOTES AND SOURCES

Chapter 1

1. Lewis B. Smedes, Forgive and Forget / Healing the Hurts We Don't Deserve (New York: Simon & Schuster, 1984) Pages 12 and 18.

2. Alan Cohen, The Dragon Doesn't Live Here Anymore (New Jersey: Alan Cohen Publications, 1981) Page 318.

3. Sidney Simon, Forgiveness (New York: Warner Books, 1990) Page 43.

Chapter 3

1. Lewis B. Smedes, Forgive and Forget / Healing the Hurts We Don't Deserve (New York: Simon & Schuster, 1984) Page 39.

Chapter 4

1. Ashleigh Brilliant, Syndicated Cartoonist.

Chapter 5

1. Lewis B. Smedes, Forgive and Forget / Healing the Hurts We Don't Deserve (New York: Simon & Schuster, 1984) Page 141.

Chapter 6
1. Sidney Simon, Forgiveness (New York: Warner Books, 1990) Page 95.

Chapter 7

1 Sidney Simon, Forgiveness (New York: Warner Books, 1990) Page 21.